NATIONAL PARKS

REDWOOD

Neil Purslow

MEDIA ENHANCED BOOKS
AV2 BY WEIGL
ADDED VALUE • AUDIO VISUAL
www.av2books.com

Published by AV^2 by Weigl
350 5th Avenue, 59th Floor
New York, NY 10118
Website: www.av2books.com

Library of Congress Control Number: 2019938448

ISBN 978-1-7911-1074-1 (hardcover)
ISBN 978-1-7911-1075-8 (softcover)
ISBN 978-1-7911-1076-5 (multi-user eBook)
ISBN 978-1-7911-1077-2 (single-user eBook)

Printed in Guangzhou, China
1 2 3 4 5 6 7 8 9 0 23 22 21 20 19

062019
311018

Project Coordinator Heather Kissock
Designers Tammy West, Ana Maria Vidal, Terry Paulhus

Photo Credits
Weigl acknowledges Getty Images, Alamy, and iStock as its primary photo suppliers for this title.

CONTENTS

A Forest of Giants

On the western shores of North America, along the coast of the Pacific Ocean, some trees grow taller than a 35-story building. These giant trees are called coast redwoods. Some of the tallest redwoods are in northern California in Redwood National Park. They can grow to be more than 360 feet (110 meters) tall.

Redwood National Park was created in 1968 to protect the redwood forest and its rivers, streams, and seashore. The park was expanded in 1978, and again in 2005. Redwood National Park now covers more than 112,500 acres (45,530 hectares).

The **oldest** known coast redwood was cut down in California in 1933. It was **2,200 years old**.

Redwood National Park preserves about **50 miles** (80 kilometers) of Pacific Ocean coastline.

The movies *Return of the Jedi* and *Jurassic Park 2: The Lost World* **included scenes** from Redwood National Park.

Redwood trees can grow 100 feet (30 m) in their first 50 years.

The park is about half the size of New York City. It contains 45 percent of the original redwood forest that remains in California today. Redwood National Park is also a **UNESCO World Heritage Site**.

Many rhododendrons bloom pink flowers among the redwood trees from mid-May into June.

MAP OF CALIFORNIA

Where in the World?

Coast redwoods flourish from central California to southern Oregon. They are only found within 30 miles (48 km) of the coast. The moisture they need to grow tall comes from the Pacific Ocean as fog in summer and rain in winter.

One-third of Redwood National Park is made up of **old-growth forests**. These ancient forests have remained undisturbed by humans. Everything is important in the old-growth forest's **ecosystem**, whether it is alive or dead. For instance, the dead trees and fallen logs on the ground provide homes to wildlife and plants.

The other two-thirds of the park include forests that have been affected by humans in the past. In the 1850s, logging provided raw materials to settlers, and gold was discovered at Gold Bluffs Beach along the Trinity River. The trees that were damaged by loggers and miners are now being replaced.

Ferns and a variety of shrubs grow in the understory beneath the looming redwoods, close to the ground.

PUZZLER

Redwood National Park is just one of the places where redwoods grow along the Pacific coast. There are three state parks as well.

Q: Research where each of these parks is located. Then, from north to south, match the name of the park with the number on the map.

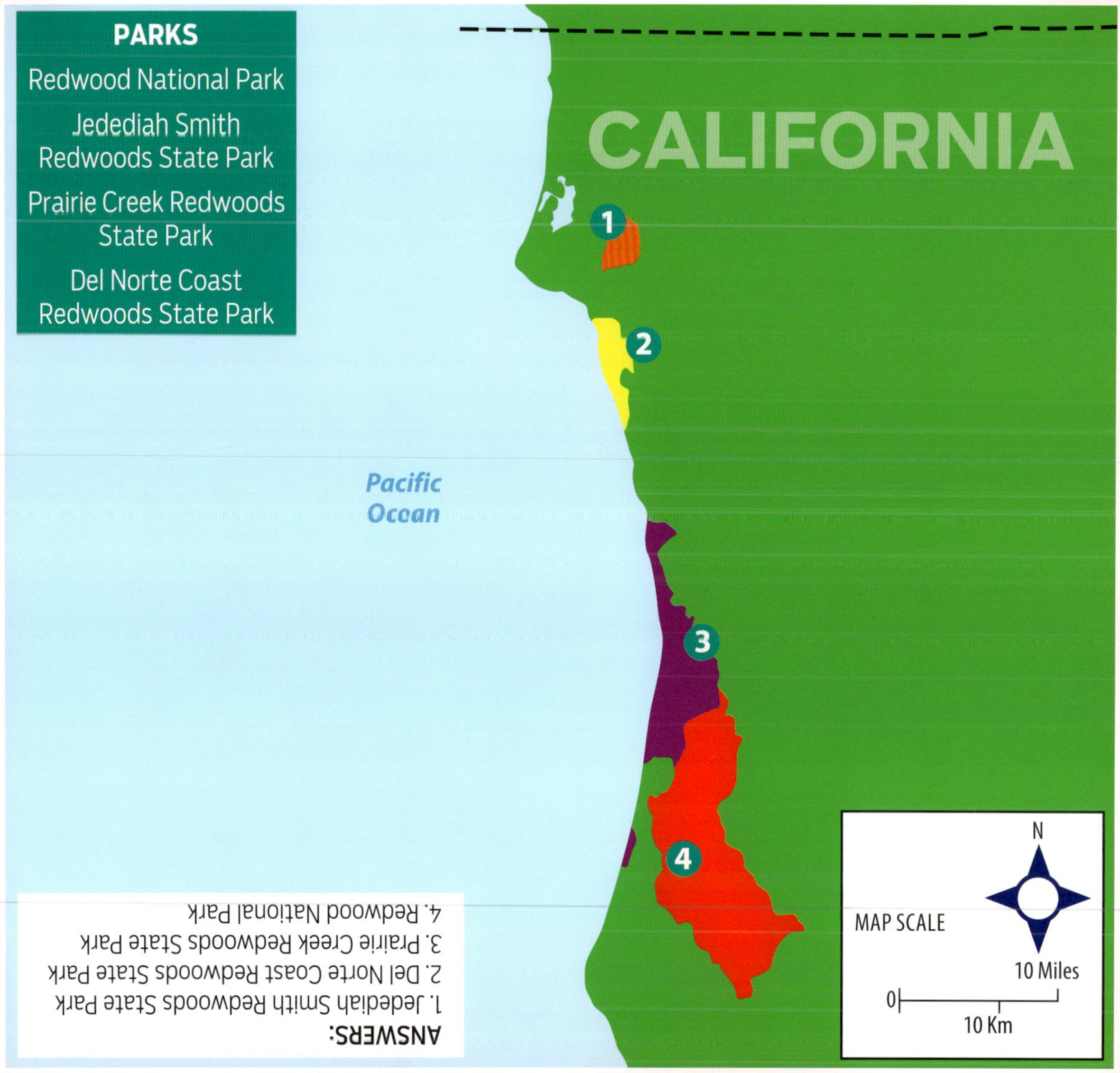

A Trip Back in Time

Many visitors to Redwood National Park feel like they are stepping back in time. Some even imagine dinosaurs rumbling through the forests. These forests have remained unchanged for millions of years. **Fossils** found in this area have shown that relatives of today's coast redwoods grew during the Jurassic Period. The Jurassic Period occurred between 144 and 208 million years ago, when dinosaurs roamed Earth.

Redwoods have thrived along the Pacific coast for 20 million years. The coast redwood has been able to survive in this area for so long because the climate here has remained much the same for millions of years. Cool, moist air from the Pacific Ocean keeps the trees and soil damp, even during summer droughts.

Fog happens on an almost daily basis at Redwood National Park because the warm inland temperatures meet the cool ocean temperatures along the California coast.

WHY DO COAST REDWOODS GROW TALL?

Exactly why coast redwoods grow so tall is a mystery. The possible reasons for why they grow so tall can also be related to why they can be so old. Scientists have developed theories on their growth.

The trees have a built-in **resistance** to natural enemies. These enemies include diseases, insects, and fires. Coast redwoods contain large quantities of tannin, a chemical that helps them resist disease and insect damage. Damage from fire is also rare because trees are protected by their thick bark and their leaves are so high above the ground.

Redwoods regenerate easily. Most trees only grow from seeds that fall onto the surface of the forest. Coast redwoods can sprout from stumps or root systems of redwoods that have fallen down.

The trees live in a healthy ecosystem. This ecosystem includes rich soil, plants, animals, and up to 140 inches (356 centimeters) of rain each year. The mild climate, with temperatures between 45° and 61° Fahrenheit (7° to 16° Celsius), also helps.

The tallest known redwood tree changes often, due to new trees growing and old trees breaking.

Plants in the Ancient Forests

Many plants besides the coast redwood grow in the ancient forests of Redwood National Park. These include spruce, hemlock, and Douglas fir trees. Smaller plants also grow in the park, such as berry bushes, sword ferns, and wildflowers.

Most of the larger trees have tops that have been damaged by the wind. These tall trees generally have fewer branches. Sometimes, the trees in Redwood National Park can be damaged by salt spray from the ocean. The trees grow best in groups, where they protect each other from salt and wind.

The leaves on the trees create a canopy above the forest. This canopy stops sunlight from reaching the floor of the forest. It also keeps the forest floor cool. These dark, cool conditions allow few plants to grow. One plant that grows well here is the rhododendron. Its colorful flowers brighten the gloom of the forest.

Lupines are found most often in the open, grassy areas of the park and closer to the coast. Their flowers can be white, or light or dark purple.

COAST REDWOODS

The scientific name for the coast redwood is *sequoia sempervirens*. Just as the name redwood implies, the wood of this tree is red. Coast redwoods are among the oldest living things on Earth. They live for about 600 years. The coast redwood is the tallest known plant in the world. It is also the fastest growing conifer, or cone-bearing tree, in North America. Surprisingly, its seed is no bigger than a tomato seed.

The root system of a coast redwood is very shallow. The roots are no deeper than 10 to 13 feet (3 to 4 m). This is unusual because of the tree's great height. Most trees and plants have **taproots**, but the redwood does not. Redwood trees grow well in groups. This allows the root systems to grow together, which provides support.

Coast Redwood Facts	
Oldest	2,200 years
Heaviest	1.6 million pounds (725,750 kilograms)
Tallest	367.8 feet (112.1 m)
Average Diameter of Trunk	22 feet (6.7 m)
Average Thickness of Bark	12 inches (30 cm)
Average Length of Needles	0.5 to 1 inch (1.3 to 2.5 cm)

Mature redwoods can move hundreds of gallons (liters) of water from their roots to their top branches every day.

Animals of Redwood

Many different animals are native to Redwood National Park. They range from black bears and bald eagles to starfish. Some threatened and endangered **species** live in the park. They rely on the old-growth forests, open prairies, rivers, and coastline for survival. Wildlife in the park is protected. Hunting is not allowed at any time, and fishing is only permitted in certain areas.

One of the largest animals in Redwood National Park is the Roosevelt elk. The elk were named after President Theodore Roosevelt, who helped save these animals from extinction. The elk herds have now grown to a healthy size in California.

Marine mammals, such as sea lions and gray whales, are often spotted swimming by the beaches. Pelicans, ospreys, and gulls nest and fish nearby. Anemones and crabs live in tide pools along the park's coast.

Roosevelt elk live in the forest, grassland, and prairie habitats within the park.

THE BANANA SLUG

Banana slugs are members of the **mollusk** family. They are the second largest slug species in the world and can grow up to 7 inches (20 cm) long. Their name comes from their color, which looks like a banana with black spots.

The banana slug lives only in moist forest floors along the Pacific coast of North America. Mushrooms are one of its favorite foods. It also eats animal droppings, leaves, and dead plants.

Banana slugs produce a protective coating called slime. This allows the slugs to travel over sharp objects unharmed. After climbing up trees, slugs can drop down quickly on a string of slime.

Banana slugs can travel 6 inches (15 cm) per minute.

The First Explorers

Some **historians** believe that European explorers saw the coast redwood forests for the first time in the 1500s. Written records from those early adventures are often missing or unclear. This makes it difficult to confirm which explorer first visited the forest. Many believe that those early explorers sailed past the forests, but did not land.

Jedediah Smith was the first explorer of European descent to travel overland through the southwest to what is now California. Smith was a hunter, trapper, and fur trader from New York. In 1828, Jedediah and his men camped atop a high ridge, covered in Douglas fir, spruce, and coast redwoods. They could see the waters of the Pacific Ocean. In the morning, they headed toward the ocean, but it took them 10 days to get there because of the tangled undergrowth and fallen logs. They were also slowed by fog and rain that made the mud on the forest floor slippery and dangerous.

Sir Francis Drake, a seaman from England, sailed around the globe and claimed the land that is now California for England in 1579. He was later awarded a knighthood by Queen Elizabeth I.

BIOGRAPHY

Jedediah Smith (1799–1831)

When Jedediah Smith was young, he read a copy of the journals of the explorers Lewis and Clark. They inspired him to travel in the wilderness. At the age of 22, Smith joined an expedition along the Missouri River to trap beavers. Soon after the ship left the dock, its mast struck a branch. The boat turned sideways and was swept under the water.

This setback did not stop Smith. Over the next eight years, he traveled through the central Rockies, down to the area now called Arizona, and across the Mojave Desert. He eventually arrived in present-day California.

In the spring of 1831, Jedediah made one more expedition. He traveled to the southwest. While looking for water on the Santa Fe Trail, he was killed by Comanche warriors.

During one of his travels west, Jedediah Smith was attacked by a grizzly bear but survived.

FACTS OF LIFE

Born: January 6, 1799

Hometown: Bainbridge, New York

Occupation: Soldier, explorer, hunter, fur trader

Died: May 27, 1831

THE BIG PICTURE

At least 12 species of redwoods have been found as fossils in Europe, Asia, and North America. Scientists believe redwoods were common in these areas until about 20 million years ago. Then, most of the redwood trees were destroyed when giant glaciers, or rivers of ice, migrated south during the Ice Age, which lasted until about 10,000 years ago. Only the trees located in the warmest climates survived. Today, there are only three species of redwoods remaining.

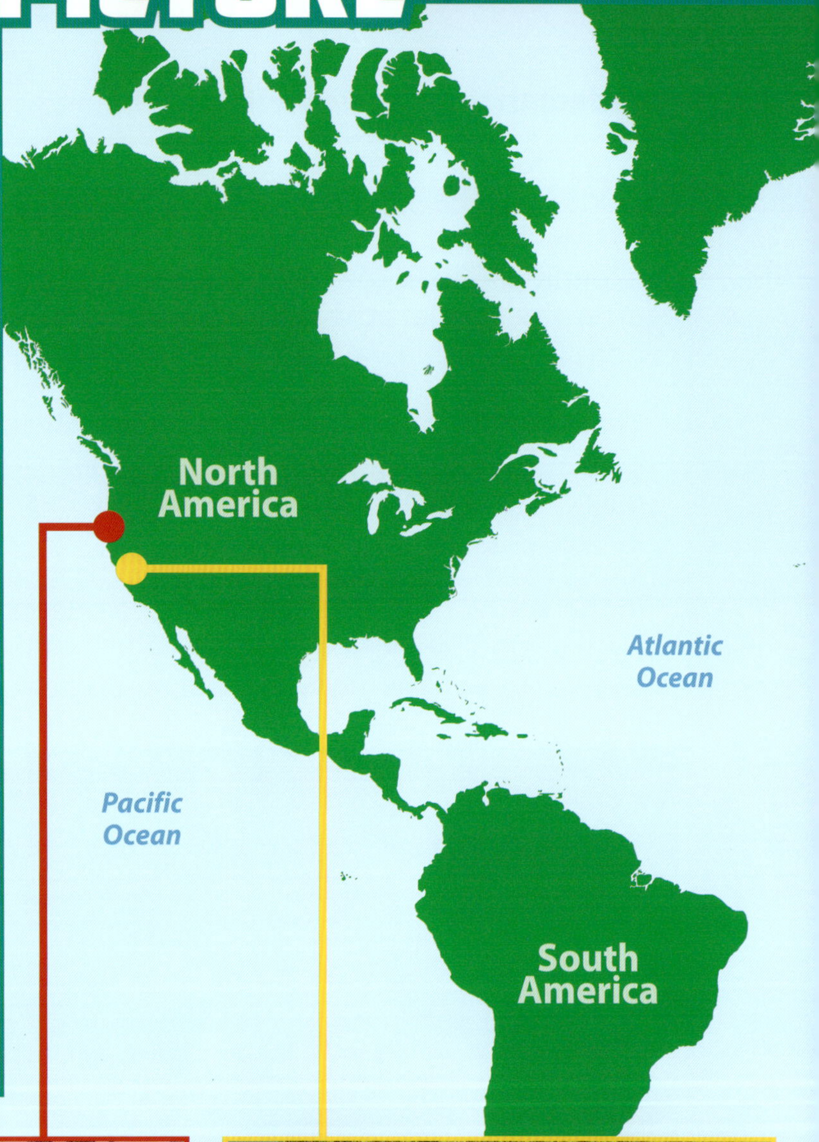

Coast Redwoods
These redwoods are the tallest of the redwoods.

Giant Sequoias
These are the massive redwoods. Their diameter can be up to 30 feet (9 m).

Dawn Redwoods
These redwoods are smaller than the other redwoods and are found only in China.

Early People of the Forests

Native Americans made the redwood forests their home for thousands of years before European explorers arrived. Many lived in small villages along the coast and major rivers. Their food sources included deer, elk, nuts, berries, and seeds. They also fished in the ocean, rivers, and streams.

The area now called Redwood National Park was inhabited by several different Native American groups. The Tolowa lived in the north, while the Yurok resided in the central part of the region. The Chilula lived inland. They all lived in harmony with nature. Nature provided them with food, clothing, housing, and transportation.

Life for these groups changed when gold miners and loggers arrived. The Native Americans were forced to leave so the newcomers could mine for gold and log the trees. If the Native Americans refused to leave their land, they were often killed by the miners and loggers instead.

Today, the Yurok are the largest group of Native Americans in California. More than 5,000 of them live in the state.

USING NATURE TO SURVIVE

Native Americans adapted to their environment. They used the materials they found in the forests to build homes and to help them hunt and fish. They also found food, such as nuts and berries, from other plants growing nearby.

Homes in this region were usually built of planks split from fallen redwoods. Native Americans believed that a house was a living being. They saw the redwood planks that formed the house as the body of one of the Spirit Beings. Spirit Beings were believed to be a godly race that existed before the time of humans.

The Yurok were dependent on water. Each family had a redwood canoe that they used to catch fish and eels. Not only was the wood plentiful, it also resisted insect damage and rotting. Trees that had been damaged by lightning or strong winds were used for canoe-making. Often, the logs would be left to dry in a cool, shady place for up to a year. When carving began, the hard center of the tree became the bottom of the canoe.

The Yurok lived along the Trinity and Klamath Rivers in what is now California. They caught fish such as salmon and sturgeon for food.

TIMELINE

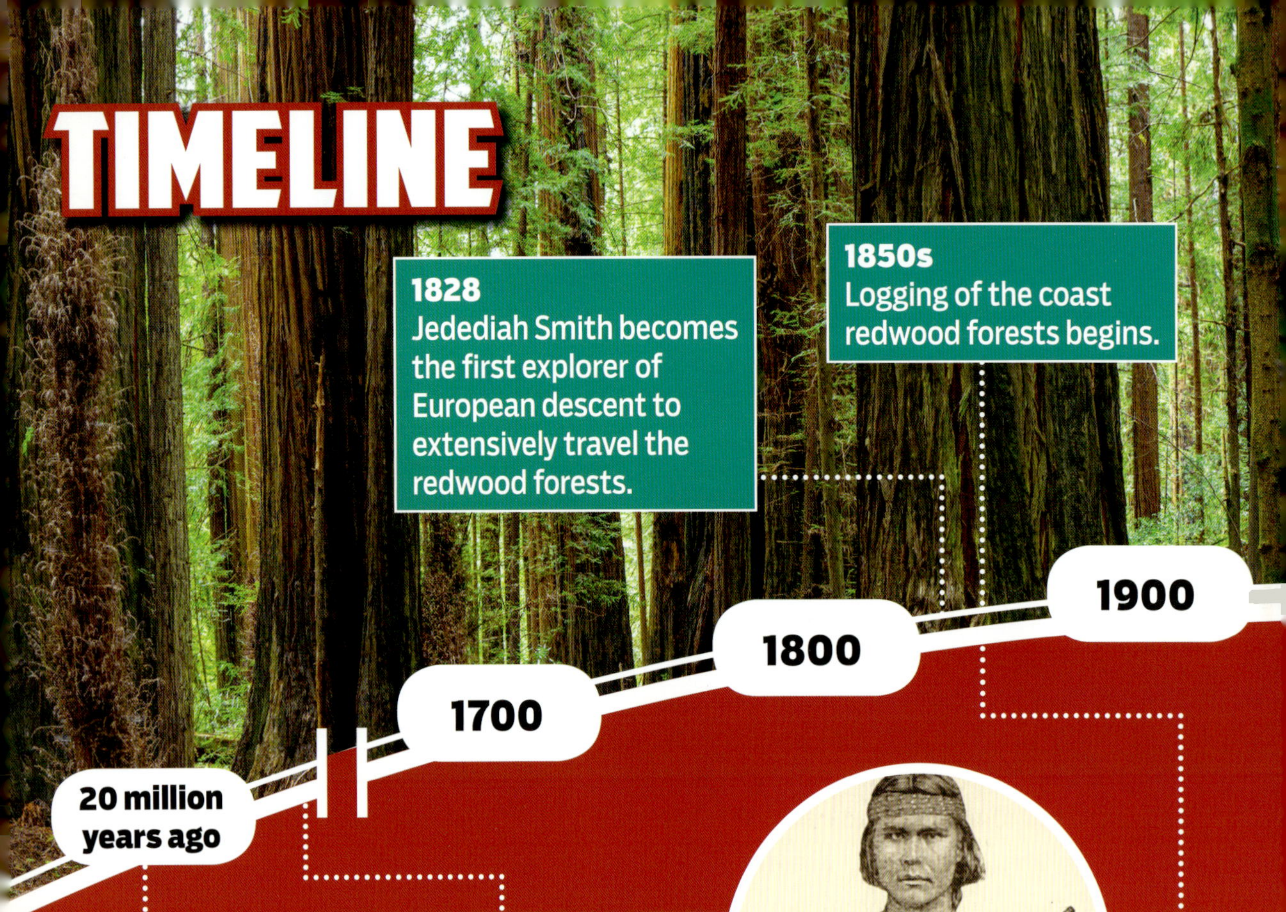

20 million years ago

1700

1800

1900

20 million years ago
The earliest coast redwoods begin growing on the west coast of North America.

3,000 years ago
Native Americans begin living in the redwood forests.

1828
Jedediah Smith becomes the first explorer of European descent to extensively travel the redwood forests.

1850
Gold is found along Trinity River, prompting a gold rush in the redwood forest.

1850s
Logging of the coast redwood forests begins.

1980s
Redwood National Park is named a World Heritage Site and an International **Biosphere** Reserve by UNESCO.

2018
Redwood National Park celebrates its 50th anniversary, as well as the 100th anniversary of the Save-the-Redwoods League. The League is an important partner of the park.

1925 **1950** **1975** **2000**

1918
The Save-the-Redwoods League is established.

1968
Redwood National Park is created by the U.S. Congress.

1994
The Jedediah Smith, Del Norte Coast, and Prairie Creek Redwoods State Parks are combined with Redwood National Park.

KEY ISSUE

LOGGING THE REDWOODS

When settlers moved west in the 1800s, they needed raw material for building homes and businesses. Logging companies followed the settlers westward. With demand high, many companies struggled to deliver timber to settlers. Timber harvesting quickly became the top industry in the west.

Coast redwoods provided an easy supply of wood. The size and straightness of the huge trees made them excellent for timber. The redwoods were known for being durable and easy to use. By 1853, nine sawmills were located in Eureka, California. Large-scale logging was everywhere. At first, axes and saws were used to bring down the trees. Then, improved technology allowed more trees to be harvested in less time. Moving the massive logs to the mills also became easier as trains replaced horses and oxen.

The once large forests of coast redwoods began disappearing rapidly. The 2 million acres (809,400 ha) of old-growth forests were becoming much smaller. Today, only 85,000 acres (34,400 ha) of old-growth redwood forests remain. Of that area, 55 percent is outside Redwood National Park.

Should the remaining old-growth forests outside the park be protected?

Yes	No
When ancient trees are cut down, it takes 600 years for them to be replaced. Countless animal species may be wiped out when the trees are removed.	The number of humans living on the west coast of North America continues to grow. Their need for building materials, including wood, has to be met.
Preserving the forests and establishing parks, hiking trails, and other tourist activities will provide jobs to the region.	Harvesting timber and replanting areas that have been cut down also brings industry and jobs to the region.
Replanting with new trees replaces the trees that have been removed, but old-growth forests can never be returned to their original condition.	Coast redwoods are a renewable resource. After trees have been removed, new ones can be planted.
The loss of trees and undergrowth can cause soil erosion. Damage from erosion can be extensive.	Clearing land for logging roads provides access to remote areas.

Logging had removed nearly 90 percent of the original redwoods by the 1960s.

Natural Attractions

At all times of the year, visitors can explore and enjoy the natural wonders of Redwood National Park. Most tourists visit the park in summer, when the weather is the warmest. The most popular activities are backpacking, biking, hiking, boating, rafting, and horseback riding. Visitors especially enjoy being in the redwood groves in the morning, when the tall trees are surrounded by fog.

Hiking through Redwood National Park can be a breathtaking experience. The park has more than 200 miles (322 km) of trails. Some trails are down at sea level, while others climb to 3,000 feet (915 m) with wonderful views. The trails weave through beaches, prairies, and old-growth forests. Bird- and wildlife-watching are popular pastimes while hiking.

Tide pools are small areas of water caught by rocks or other items that stay behind when the ocean's tide ebbs. They can be found in several locations around Redwood National Park.

BE PREPARED

Trails in the park are accessible year-round because of the mild climate of the area. However, hikers must be careful because the trails are often wet and slippery. In winter, some trails may be difficult to use. Sturdy footwear and rain gear should be worn in the park.

When on the trails, care must be taken around some of the animals in the park. Although not seen very often, black bears roam freely in the park, especially around Redwood Creek. They enjoy eating acorns and will travel far to find them.

TIP: When camping, store certain items high off the ground so as not to attract bears. Place all food, garbage, and scented items, such as soap, toothpaste, and lotions, in a tree. Ensure they are at least 12 feet (3.6 m) up, 10 feet (3 m) out from the trunk, and 5 feet (1.5 m) down from the branch.

Mountain lions, or cougars, live in Redwood National Park. These animals prefer to avoid humans. Sometimes spotted in picnic areas and along trails and roads, mountain lions once ranged from northern Canada to South America and from coast to coast. Now, because of hunting and a loss of forests, mountain lions have a smaller range.

TIP: Although there have only been two mountain lion attacks in the park, hikers should be prepared. People should not hike alone. Children should not run ahead on trails.

Saving the Forests

At one time, 2 million acres (809,400 ha) of old-growth forests existed along the Pacific coast. When settlers came west, they needed raw materials. Coast redwoods were logged to make lumber for homes and businesses. By about 1910, the last of the old-growth forests were about to disappear. Many people did not want this to happen because fossil records showed that these trees were related to trees millions of years old.

To save the trees, a group called Save-the-Redwoods League was started in 1918. The league bought large areas of the redwood forests in order to save the trees from disappearing completely. The State of California helped the league by also buying old-growth forests. By 1960, more than 100,000 acres (40,500 ha) had been preserved.

The arrival of railways in California in the mid-1800s helped feed the demand for redwood lumber. Trains made transporting the lumber faster and easier than it had ever been before.

BECOMING A NATIONAL PARK

In 1968, the United States Congress approved 58,000 acres (23,500 ha) of the land bought by the Save-the-Redwoods League to be made into a national park. President Lyndon B. Johnson signed the law to create the park. Redwood National Park was later expanded to its present size.

In 1980, the park became a UNESCO World Heritage Site. These sites are chosen for their importance to humans. Sites include forests, mountain ranges, lakes, deserts, buildings, and cities.

In 1983, the park was named an International Biosphere Reserve by UNESCO. These reserves are created to promote a balance between humans and the biosphere. Reserves must consist of land, coast, or marine ecosystems.

A section of the park is called Lady Bird Johnson Grove. It was named after President Lyndon B. Johnson's wife, who promoted the protection of natural habitats.

WHAT HAVE YOU LEARNED?

TRUE OR FALSE?

Decide whether the following statements are true or false. If the statement is false, make it true.

1
Redwood National Park is located in northern Oregon.

2
Coast redwoods grow within 30 miles (48 km) of the Pacific Ocean.

3
The bark on a coast redwood is 36 inches (91 cm) thick.

4
Kennedy elk are the largest animals in the park.

5
Redwood National Park became an International Biosphere Reserve in 1983.

6
There have been no mountain lion attacks in the park.

ANSWERS
1. False. Redwood National Park is located in northern California. 2. True 3. False. The bark on a coast redwood is 12 inches (30 cm) thick. 4. False. Roosevelt elk are the largest animals in the park. 5. True 6. False. There have been two mountain lion attacks in the park.

SHORT ANSWER

Answer the following questions using information from the book.

1 What are the names of the state parks that also protect redwoods?

2 What are the names of the three redwood trees that grow in the world today?

3 What did Native Americans use coast redwoods for in the past?

4 What other trees grow in Redwood National Park?

5 How deep are the roots on a coast redwood?

ANSWERS
1. Jedediah Smith, Del Norte Coast, and Prairie Creek Redwoods State Parks
2. Coast redwood, giant sequoia, and dawn redwood
3. Houses and canoes
4. Spruce, hemlock, and Douglas fir
5. 10 to 13 feet (3 to 4 m)

MULTIPLE CHOICE

Choose the best answer for the following questions.

1 How many acres does Redwood National Park cover?

a. 112,500 acres (45,530 ha)
b. 212,500 acres (86,000 ha)
c. 312,500 acres (126,470 ha)
d. 412,500 acres (166,940 ha)

2 In what year was the Save-the-Redwood League formed?

a. 1828
b. 1850
c. 1918
d. 1968

3 When camping in the park, food should be:

a. placed on a picnic table away from your tent
b. placed high in a tree
c. stored in your tent
d. left on the ground

4 The diameter of the coast redwood averages:

a. 12 feet (3.7 m)
b. 16 feet (4.9 m)
c. 19 feet (5.8 m)
d. 22 feet (6.7 m)

ANSWERS
1. a 2. c 3. b 4. d

ACTIVITY

MAKING CLOUDS

Redwood National Park is usually rainy, cloudy, or foggy. This weather is part of what helps the redwood trees grow so tall. Create your own cloud, made from a collection of water droplets, with the following activity.

Materials

- Glass jar
- Sheet of black paper
- Tape
- Hot water
- Metal pan
- Match
- Ice cubes in a plastic bag

Instructions

1. Cut and tape a piece of black paper to fit halfway around the jar, leaving about 1 inch (2.5 cm) of space at the bottom half of the jar.
2. Fill the jar to the top with hot water. If an adult can boil water on a stove top or microwave oven, the results are better. Leave it for about 1 minute. Then, pour out all but about 1 inch (2.5 cm) of the water.
3. Have an adult light a match and hold it over the jar opening for a few seconds.
4. Drop the match in the water.
5. Quickly cover the jar with the metal pan.
6. Quickly place the plastic bag of ice cubes over the top of the metal pan, still covering the jar.

Results

The warm water and the match heated the air inside the jar. The warm, wet air rose up to the top of the jar and ran into the cold air just below the ice cubes. When the warm wet air met the cold wet air, they created a cloud of water droplets.

KEY WORDS

biosphere: the areas of Earth's crust and atmosphere occupied by living organisms

ecosystem: a community of organisms and the environment in which they live

fossils: imprints of prehistoric plants or animals in rocks

historians: people who study history

mollusk: a species of animal that has a soft body and no visible skeleton

old-growth forests: ancient forests that have not been damaged by humans

resistance: the ability to resist or fight off

species: a specific group of plants or animals that share the same characteristics

taproots: large, tapered roots growing downward from plants

UNESCO World Heritage Site: a place that is of natural or cultural importance to the entire world. UNESCO is an abbreviation for United Nations Educational, Scientific, and Cultural Organization.

INDEX

Log on to www.av2books.com

AV² by Weigl brings you media enhanced books that support active learning. Go to www.av2books.com, and enter the special code found on page 2 of this book. You will gain access to enriched and enhanced content that supplements and complements this book. Content includes video, audio, weblinks, quizzes, a slideshow, and activities.

AV² Online Navigation

Audio
Listen to sections o
the book read alou

Book Pages
AV² pages directly correspond to pages in the book.

Video
Watch informative video clips.

Embedded Weblinks
Gain additional information for research.

Key Words
Study vocabulary, and complete a matching word activity.

Try This!
Complete activities and hands-on experiments.

Quizzes
Test your knowledge.

Slideshow
View images and captions, and prepare a presentation.

AV² was built to bridge the gap between print and digital. We encourage you to tell us what you like and what you want to see in the future.

Sign up to be an AV² Ambassador at www.av2books.com/ambassador.

Due to the dynamic nature of the internet, some of the URLs and activities provided as part of AV² by Weigl may have changed or ceased to exist. AV² by Weigl accepts no responsibility for any such changes. All media enhanced books are regularly monitored to update addresses and sites in a timely manner. Contact AV² by Weigl at 1-866-649-3445 or av2books@weigl.com with any questions, comments, or feedback.